Thinking of You!

_____

May the God of hope fill you with all joy and peace as you trust in Him so that your heart might overflow with hope by the power of the Holy Spirit! May the joy of the Lord be the strength of your heart, today and always.

Blessings of Hope & Joy,

_____

_____

date

Romans 15:13; Nehemiah 8:10

Surprising Stories, Stirring Messages, and Refreshing Scriptures That Make the Heart Soar

heartlifters™

for Hope and Joy

LeAnn Weiss

messages by
Susan Duke

HOWARD
PUBLISHING CO.

Our purpose at Howard Publishing is to:

- *Increase faith* in the hearts of growing
  Christians
- *Inspire holiness* in the lives of believers
- *Instill hope* in the hearts of struggling people
  everywhere

Because He's coming again!

Heartlifters™ for Hope and Joy © 1999 by LeAnn Weiss
All rights reserved. Printed in Hong Kong
Published by Howard Publishing Co., Inc.
3117 North 7th Street, West Monroe, Louisiana 71291-2227

00 01 02 03 04 05 06 07 08   10 9 8 7 6 5 4 3 2

Library of Congress Cataloging-in-Publication Data
Weiss, LeAnn.
    Heartlifters for hope and joy : surprising stories, stirring
messages, and refreshing scriptures that make the heart soar / LeAnn
Weiss ; messages by Susan Duke.
        p. cm.
    ISBN 1-58229-074-1
    1. Christian life. I. Duke, Susan. II. Title.
BV4515.2.W39 1999   99-29161
242'—dc21   CIP

Personalized scriptures by LeAnn Weiss, owner of Encouragement Company
3006 Brandywine Dr., Orlando, FL 32806; (407) 898-4410

Edited by Philis Boultinghouse
Cover and interior design by LinDee Loveland

Scripture quotation from *The Holy Bible, New King James Version* (NKJV), © 1982 by Thomas Nelson, Inc.

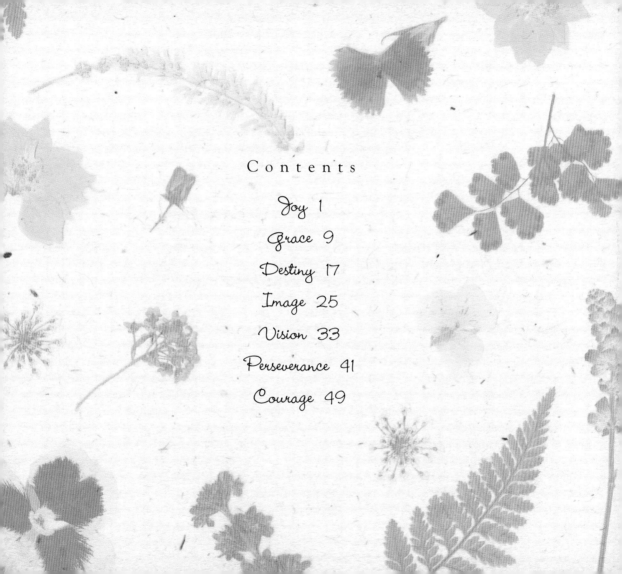

Contents

Joy is the holy fire that keeps our purpose warm and our intelligence aglow. Resolve to keep happy, and your joy and you shall form an invincible hope against difficulty.

—HELEN KELLER

Joy

As a twelve-year-old preacher's kid, Barbara Leary's happy life was interrupted when her father died suddenly. Just before his fatal heart attack, he had called from church telling her he was bringing home her favorite Black Jack gum. Barbara's close relationship with her father made losing him even more difficult.

Many years later, while driving her children to a church youth retreat, Barbara slammed on the brakes of her car when her headlights spotted a man lying in the middle of the mountainside road. Stopping to help, she was horrified to discover that the disfigured, bloodied victim was her own husband. Doctors offered little hope, labeling him "completely and totally unrehabilitable, with a life expectancy of only five years." Barbara assumed sole responsibility for raising their four boys and caring for her now-blind and disabled husband.

Her husband's first weeks out of the hospital discouraged Barbara almost to the breaking point. Although he was home and in familiar surroundings,

Joy

his memory had partially failed because of brain damage. Several months after the accident, God miraculously began healing his eyesight and memory, eventually leading to a complete recovery.

A little more than two years after her husband's near-fatal accident, Barbara's world came crashing down again when two marines knocked on her door delivering news that her eighteen-year-old son had been killed by enemy fire in Vietnam. Five years later, her timid and spiritually challenged oldest son phoned to say he had rededicated his heart to the Lord after an exciting personal revival and was on his way home from Alaska. Just a few hours later, he was tragically killed by a drunk driver.

In 1975 Barbara discovered that another son, a promising, young Christian leader, was homosexual. This news almost pushed her over the edge, filling her mind with thoughts of suicide. However, she eventually learned to "let go" and relinquish her son to God—even though her son disowned them, changed his name, and disappeared into the gay lifestyle for eleven heart-breaking years before coming back to the Lord and reestablishing contact.

In 1979, out of the blue, Barbara received a phone call from a publishing company with an unsolicited request for her to write a book about her life. Miraculously, the almost fifty-year-old housewife who hated English in high school wrote her first book, *Where Does a Mother Go to Resign?* in eight, short weeks. Without benefit of a

Joy

single writing course, she became a best-selling author, humorist, and extremely popular speaker almost overnight.

Today her audiences and readers across the country roar with belly-busting laughter, responding to her zany, off-the-wall humor and joyful outlook on life. Few eyes remain dry as she shares stories from her pain-filled past.

Barbara Johnson, a mom who at one time wanted to resign from motherhood, started Spatula Ministries in 1978 – a ministry that "peels parents off the ceiling with a spatula of love and starts them on the road to recovery."

"God held me up when my mind and emotions were blown apart by tragedy. He gave me the gift of joy, which makes it possible to share with others the good things God is going to do for them too," reflects Barbara. Looking back, Barbara never imagined that God would use her story to touch millions of hurting lives. In the world's eyes, her tragedy-filled life made her an unlikely speaker for the popular Joyful Journey tour. But Barbara realizes, "It was the countless tears that gave me credentials of true joy not dependent on my external circumstances." As a team member and key speaker with Women of Faith, she continues to speak about the joy available through Jesus Christ.

Her many best-selling books include *Stick a Geranium in Your Hat and Be Happy, Splashes of Joy from the Cesspools of Life, Boomerang Joy,* and *He's Gonna Toot and I'm Gonna Scoot.*

three

Do you know the children's song, "I've got the joy, joy, joy, joy down in my heart – down in my heart to stay"? Have you ever realized the simple truth this little song conveys? Down in your heart is where joy lives, where it finds its home – its base of operation.

Joy is not a feeling. It's a knowing. The world often confuses happiness with joy. Happiness is dependent on outward circumstances. Joy is not. You'll be faced with many situations in life that make you unhappy – things you have no control over. But trials can't rob you of your joy. It is a gift that cannot be taken away. For joy is like a natural spring that bubbles up from your innermost being. It's a continual flow of assurance from your River of Life – Jesus.

f o u r

You have a choice, an opportunity to keep your "joy light" burning in dark situations, to sit by its warm fire. And the warmth of your joy will flow into the lives of those around you, for joy is contagious.

Joy is ointment to your soul. Joy looks adversity in the eye and rests its head on God's chest. Joy, an immovable force, motivates and inspires. Jesus explained, "This is not the kind of joy the world knows," but a supernatural abiding peace. When you choose joy, you have the assurance that even the things in life that cause you pain work for your good. Choosing joy means Jesus is enough – in every trial, in every sorrow. He is the restorer and burden bearer. Joy is the fruit of our "oneness with God."

five

Joy believes that even in the midst of a storm, a rainbow will soon appear.

Joy is knowing that wherever Jesus lives, joy lives also…"down in my heart to stay."

Look for My splashes of joy...

Grace comes into the soul, as the morning sun into the world; first a dawning; then a light; and at last the sun in his full and excellent brightness.

—THOMAS ADAMS

Grace

Born March 24, 1820, she was christened Frances Jane. Her parents were alarmed when their newborn's eyes became red and inflamed. Because their family physician was unavailable, she was taken to a doctor they didn't know. They were horrified when the doctor (who turned out to be a quack) put a hot poultice on their six-week-old daughter's eyes claiming it would "draw out" the infection. The infection gradually healed, but their firstborn daughter was forever blinded.

Tragedy struck her family again later that same year when her father became chilled while working in a downpour and died a few days later. When Frances's mother had to go to work to help support her family, Frances's grandmother, Eunice, stepped in to help raise her. Sustained by her deep faith in God, Eunice taught her granddaughter that God used suffering and frustration to lead to something better. Even after Frances and her mother moved out to live on their own, Eunice continued to play a

Grace

major role in Frances's spiritual life and education.

Then one day in November of 1834, Frances's mom read of a new school for the blind. Frances later described this day as the "happiest day" of her life. The next March, when Frances was nearly fifteen, she said good-bye to her mother and headed for New York by stagecoach. The new school, one of only two such schools in the entire nation, opened new doors of opportunity for Frances. While she never became adept at Braille, she became nationally recognized as "The Blind Poetess" when her poems were published in her book, *The Blind Girl and Other Poems*.

While representing her school in its efforts to gain support for its cause, Frances entertained six U.S. presidents and inspired the nation concerning the potential of education for the blind.

Grover Cleveland, a young employee at the New York Institute for the Blind, often transcribed Frances's poems as she dictated. The friendship forged between them continued through his presidency.

In 1858, she married Alexander Van Alstyne, a blind musician, and they left the Institute to begin a new life together. Sadly, their only child died in infancy. At William Bradbury's encouragement, Frances Jane turned her attention to hymnwriting. Her phenomenal memory, which helped her memorize many books of

Grace

the Bible as a small child, greatly aided her songwriting, as she was unable to refer back to her written work. She never earned more than four hundred dollars a year, and she gave away most of her income not needed for basic needs. Living in very humble means herself, she spent countless hours ministering to the down-and-outs in street missions in the slums of New York.

Frances Jane classified her growth in grace as "very slow from the beginning." But she learned to view even her blindness as a gift from God. Realizing that the physician's blunder prepared her to write hymns, she remarkably stated: "If perfect earthly sight were offered to me tomorrow, I would not accept it." She realized, "I could not have written thousands of hymns…if I had been hindered by the distractions of seeing all the interesting and beautiful objects that would have been presented to my notice."

Her hymns became favorites at D. L. Moody's revivals. Some of her better known hymns include "Blessed Assurance," "Safe in the Arms of Jesus," "Praise Him, Praise Him," "Close to Thee," "All the Way My Savior Leads Me," and "To God Be the Glory."

Near the end of her life, Fanny J. Crosby, who wrote nearly nine thousand hymns under hundreds of pseudonyms, penned the words "And I shall see Him face to face and tell the story – saved by Grace."

$\mathcal{W}$e will all go through trials we think we can't bear – when grief is too hard to comprehend, when even words from a friend can't distill our pain.

When all hope is gone, all dreams are lost, and your heart is empty, grace makes its entrance. It covers you physically, like a cocoon in God's waiting room. It wraps you in a blanket, holds you firmly, and speaks through the silence... "You are not alone."

Sometimes, in the midst of trials, we are called to be a showcase of God's grace. When everything around us is sinking sand, we can stand on our Rock, our unmovable source of strength, and display to all onlookers that our God is sufficient to sustain us.

twelve

God's infinite grace gives us wings to fly, like the eagle, above the clouds, in the eye of storm – steady, sure, and confident that, while the storm rages, we are "grace insured."

Grace is freedom – freedom to be forgiven, freedom to forgive. Grace gives us permission to be ourselves, authentic, real, without pretense.

Grace throws off every mask and says, "There's no need to hide." Grace replaces fear with joy, acceptance, and delight.

Grace is love personified. We can't earn it. We don't always deserve it. It's a free gift, given with "no strings attached." Imagine you were given an anonymous gift of a

Grace

million dollars and all you had to do was go to the bank and claim it. You wouldn't have to think of a way to pay it back. Even to try would be an insult.

God's gift of grace is unconditional, unmerited favor. There is nothing you can ever do to make God love you any more than He already does.

When God sent His son to die on the cross, grace was born. Isn't it amazing?

My grace is more than sufficient for you...

We never know how high we are
till we are called to rise. And then,
if we are true to plan, our statures
touch the skies.

—EMILY DICKINSON

Destiny

When the hospital maternity ward misplaced Madeline's nametag, her father easily identified her by her long, narrow feet and high-pitched voice.

At three years old, Madeline lay motionless in another hospital bed, a victim of spinal meningitis. When doctors grimly told the family that they had done everything "medically possible," Madeline's mother prayed by her bedside all night. Surprised to find young Madeline doing better the next morning, the doctors upgraded her survival chances to fifty-fifty. Still cautious, the doctors warned that even if she lived, she would be mentally retarded and physically handicapped. Her mom responded with a smiling confidence that the Great Physician was looking after her Madeline.

Madeline survived. At age six, when she prayed, asking Jesus into her heart, something inside her began to change. Although Madeline struggled physically and mentally over the next fourteen years, even frail and anemic at times, she sensed that God wanted her to do something big

Destiny

for Him. That sense of destiny gave her hope and sustained her through childhood trials. When she was only six years old, her parents divorced. She lived in impoverished projects until age nine when her mother remarried, and she faced frequent racial prejudice.

In 1963, when President John F. Kennedy unveiled the National Physical Fitness Awards Program for schools, Madeline, a shy high-school student, took the new required test and topped national athletic standards. Almost overnight, she found herself playing varsity volleyball, track, and basketball and began breaking out of her introverted shell. Who would guess that within five years, Madeline would be in the Olympic Village to compete against the best athletes in the world?

At the '68 Olympics, Madeline set a world record in the 800-meter run, becoming the first U.S. female ever to win a gold medal in that event. Her 1976 record-setting time distinguished Madeline as the first American female to run the 800 meters in under two minutes. At the '72 Olympics, Madeline was on the silver medal 4 x 400 meter relay team. In top physical condition for the '80 Olympics, she supported the U.S. boycott of the Moscow games. She held the American outdoor record for the women's 800 for fifteen years, running it as fast as 1:57.9. In 1984, she was inducted into the USA Track and Field Hall of Fame.

Destiny

Today, four-time Olympian and recording artist Madeline Manning Mims continues to go for the gold on a higher level. Founder and president of Ambassadorship, Inc., a not-for-profit organization based out of Tulsa, Oklahoma, Madeline boldly leads teams of athletes and youth in sharing the love of Christ with young people on the mission field through sports and performing arts. She disciples leaders and works with Christian sports groups, including Fellowship of Christian Athletes, Athletes in Action, and Athletes International Ministries. Madeline served as an Olympic Chaplain at the 1988 Seoul Olympic Games, the 1992 Barcelona Olympic Games, and the 1996 Atlanta Olympic Games.

Madeline reflects, "My God set a destiny for me greater than I could have ever asked for and far beyond my dreams. He established my goings and centered my hope of glory in Christ Jesus."

It visited you in wishes and dreams when you were a child. It whispered your name that time you wondered why you were born. Then boldly it called you to a place deep inside where you heard its effervescent endorsement loud and clear.

That's when you knew. It didn't matter what roadblocks you might encounter along the way. It didn't matter what circumstance might try to prevent you from believing. It didn't even matter if anyone else believed. You realized God had a purpose for your life – that with Him at the helm, you could make a difference.

Joseph's destiny took him from the pit to the palace. Sarah carried and delivered a patriarch when she was well past childbearing age. To his family, David was a shepherd boy, but God knew he was destined to be a king. Rahab, voted least likely to succeed, saved herself and her household when Jericho fell.

From the passerby who pulls a child from a burning building and becomes a hero, to the teacher, astronaut, doctor, nurse, Olympian, or housewife who creates a haven for those she loves, our destinies are fulfilled in many ways in our lifetime.

There was no mistake. The angels danced the day you were born. You were in God's plan before the foundation of the earth. He planned the year, the month, the day, and the very moment you would make your unique entrance into this world. You are a Designer's original. God lit the torch and equipped you with everything needed to run the race. Go for the gold. Fulfill your destiny. One day He'll be passing out medals.

I have plans for you...

You are valuable just because you exist. Not because of what you do or what you have done, but simply because you are.

—MAX LUCADO

Image

"Doctor, I have come to tell you that I am expecting a child and you are the father," confessed seventeen-year-old Sarah Wade. When the doctor told her he was engaged to be married, she asked him to do whatever was medically necessary to stop the birth, thus saving their child from disgrace.

Refusing to abort his own flesh, the country doctor argued that illegitimacy wouldn't necessarily handicap their child, as she feared. Ironically he said, "This child may be a son, and for all we know, he might some day be governor of Tennessee."

On October 13, 1870, unwanted Bennie Wade was born in a cabin in the foothills of the Great Smoky Mountains. Shortly after his birth, he and his mother left Newport, Tennessee, moving from one place to another before ending up in the slums of Knoxville. Bennie's only playground was dirty streets and alleys. Other children often tormented the fatherless boy with cruel names.

Image

When Bennie was seven years old, in 1878, his mother dressed him in his least-worn clothes and instructed him to leave with the lady and little girl at their door. Bennie was too young to realize that his mother was sending him away for good. One day, while living at St. John's orphanage, he was introduced to Dr. D. L. Hooper, the father Bennie never knew existed. After the death of Dr. Hooper's adopted infant, he learned the whereabouts of his natural son and brought him home on November 9, 1879.

Back in Newport with his father and stepmother, Ben was again the subject of salacious gossip and taunting. Motivated by the belief that sensible people might appraise him for his character rather than his accidental birth, he worked hard to become a leader. At age eleven, Ben felt stirred to come forward during evangelistic meetings at a Baptist church, but the shame of his birth stopped him. Finally, at age fifteen, he realized that he was loved and wanted by God. That night, as he professed his faith in Christ, an enormous burden lifted from his mind and soul, freeing him from his past.

Ben embarked on a career in law but soon added politics to his passions. Shortly after his twenty-second birthday, he was elected to the state legislature and headed to Nashville. Ben was reelected in 1894. When the Spanish-American War broke out in the spring of 1898, he left his flourishing Newport law firm to serve as a commissioned army captain. After the war, Ben returned to private law until he

was appointed assistant U.S. attorney for the eastern district of Tennessee. He resigned in 1910 to run for governor.

Despite the opposition's attempts to make his scandalous birth an issue, Ben was elected governor of Tennessee in 1910 and reelected for a second term in 1912. Recognized for his integrity and fairness, Governor Ben W. Hooper led prohibition efforts, passed child labor laws, started compulsory school, and helped children, veterans, and widows. Serving during one of the most turbulent periods in the history of Tennessee politics, he worked hard to reduce election fraud and corruption. His speeches, correspondence, and actions reflected his faith.

Following his governorship, Ben became a judge and was later appointed by President Warren G. Harding to the U.S. Railway Labor Board. As chairman, he was credited with averting a national strike of railroad employees, which could have crippled the U.S. economic structure.

$\mathcal{I}$ heard the story of a young boy who, because of his life's humiliating circumstances, felt the bitter sting of rejection from all who knew him. He felt disgraced, even when he went to church. He purposely slipped into the back of the church late and left early to avoid the harsh glare of judgment. One day, the preacher concluded his sermon abruptly and said the benediction before the young boy reached the back door. As he squirmed through the crowded aisle, suddenly, he felt a hand on his shoulder. It was the preacher.

"Who are you?" the preacher asked boldly. "Whose son are you?"

The boy lowered his head in shame, but the preacher gently tipped the boy's chin upward and smiled at him. "I know who you are. I see the family resemblance. You are God's son," the preacher said. He patted the boy on the back and told him, "You have a great inheritance. Go and claim it."

After becoming a prominent man in society, he often shared this story, declaring the preacher's words as the most important ever spoken to him – words that forever changed his image and destiny.

Encouraging words are keys that unlock prison doors of the past. They are soft rain to a parched soul, a rainbow's promise in the darkest storms of life, a lifeboat in a raging sea of despair. Words are a lighthouse that guides us through the fog of uncertain vision.

twenty-nine

Image

You've been chosen, adopted by a Father who gives you life through His words. He pats you on the shoulder, lifts your head, and tells you that you belong to Him.

thirty

You've been chosen by Me...

$\mathcal{O}$nly those who can see the invisible can do the impossible.

—JOHN AVANZINI

Vision

As a high-school senior, Henrietta walked down her church aisle, responding to a challenge for full-time Christian service. Her heart's desire was to serve the Lord in whatever work He ordained for her.

But Henrietta's vision began to deteriorate, and doctors cautioned her that she would be blind by the time she was thirty if she continued studying and reading. Undaunted, she completed her college education and became a chemistry teacher.

Henrietta believed in "blooming where God had planted her" and became the director of Christian Education at the First Presbyterian Church in Hollywood, California, in 1928. "To know Christ and to make Him known" was Henrietta's focus while teaching the college department. Sunday-school attendance increased from four hundred fifty to more than four thousand in two and a half years under her leadership.

Although Henrietta struggled with her physical sight all her life, her spiritual vision was keen – for her focus was ever

Vision

on God. With a God-sized perspective of life, she believed in beginning with current circumstances and adding a vision of what God can do to create an unbeatable combination. "When I consider my ministry," she said, "I think of the world. Anything less than that would not be worthy of Christ nor His will for my life." More than four hundred of the young people she taught entered full-time Christian service.

In 1947, Bill, an agnostic convert, was one of the young people who pledged himself to "absolute consecration to Christ" through Henrietta's discipleship. She also led Vonette, who would become Bill's wife and life part-ner, to a personal relationship with Jesus. Henrietta was instrumental in cultivating Bill's God-given vision to help fulfill the Great Commission for this generation.

In 1951, Bill and his wife, Vonette, launched a ministry from the UCLA campus geared at winning and discipling the students of the world for Christ. Henrietta, Billy Graham, Dawson Trotman, and others agreed to serve on the advisory board. In 1965, Bill authored *The Four Spiritual Laws*, introducing tens of millions of people worldwide to the gospel in a simple, straightforward presentation.

Today, Campus Crusade for Christ International, the ministry cofounded by Bill and Vonette Bright, is active on more than 1,069 campuses. The ministry

Vision

employs more than 19,000 staff members and 281,000 trained associates and volunteers who have established ministries in 172 countries and protectorates. More than 2.5 billion people have been exposed to the good news of the gospel through various departments of this ministry in the last half-century. More than 83 million decisions have been made through the *Jesus* film, which has been translated into 484 languages with 250 more in process. And it all began with a woman's vision to do God's will wherever He placed her.

Long before her 1963 death, Dr. Henrietta C. Mears realized that many people are serving on mission fields around the world because she simply yielded to God's will, ministering where He had placed her. Wisely, she encouraged, "Have unlimited vision under God, have enthusiasm and faith in what God can do. Without this vision you will become discouraged with the situation at hand; with it you will know that with God all things are possible."

Imagine finding a plain brown box filled with pieces of a jigsaw puzzle. As you sort through countless pieces, you find yourself wondering what picture will appear when they are all connected. One or two pieces will not reveal the mystery. Yet, one by one, while fitting each jagged fragment, an image begins to form. Soon, you begin to see – at least in part – what the fitted pieces will finally become. Not until every one of them is set firmly in place will the full picture emerge.

Do you sometimes wonder where all the pieces of your life fit together in God's plan for you? You may get anxious or impatient while trying to see the whole picture. And there will be times when a fragment of your life doesn't quite seem to fit what you'd envisioned or hoped.

But don't lose heart. God sees amazing potential in you!
And you can rest assured that He is carefully placing each
piece of your life's puzzle into place. His dreams for you are
even bigger than your own! He already sees the end result.

Hold on to the vision God has given you. Don't let the
murky waters of distractions cloud your view of what He has
created you to be. The goals you may have put on the shelf,
the promises to which you have held fast, are all vital parts of
God's bigger picture.

In God's perfect timing, His unlimited vision for your life
will reach farther, higher, and wider than you could ever
dream. So enjoy the mountainous view from His perspective

thirty-seven

– far beyond the jagged pieces of this world's limited sight to the completeness of eternal glory.

I ordained all your days...

You may have to fight
a battle more than once to
win it.

—MARGARET THATCHER

Perseverance

He was eulogized as the "grandest figure on the crowded canvas of the drama of the nineteenth century." However, much of his life seemed anything but grand.

When he was nine, "milk sickness" – caused by consuming milk from cattle that had eaten the poisonous white snakeroot – killed his mother. After their mother's death, he and his sister found their greatest comfort in the pages of her Bible, which she had taught them to read. But his mother's death was not the only one he endured. His sister died years later in childbirth. He was grief-stricken again when his young son died just before his fourth birthday. His "hardest trial" came over a decade later when his favorite son, who aspired to be a preacher, died when a severe cold turned into fever.

Although he received only one year of formal education, he was a firm believer in its value, saying that it was "the most important subject, we, as a people, can be engaged in." Diligently dedicated to educating himself, he borrowed books

Perseverance

wherever he could and read them cover to cover.

His passion to make a difference in his community led him to pursue a political career. Humbly acknowledging his inexperience when he announced his candidacy for the state legislature, he said, "I am young and unknown to you. I was born and have ever remained in the most humble walks of life." Despite his diligent campaigning, he finished eighth in a race with thirteen candidates. To his defeat he responded, "I have been too familiar with disappointments to be very much chagrined."

However, his disappointments compounded. When the store he owned in partnership failed and his partner died, he was left solely responsible for an astronomical debt. For seventeen years, he sacrificed, sometimes working several jobs. Gradually, he repaid every penny of the eleven hundred dollars he owed. Then when his fiancée, Ann Rutledge, died at only twenty-two, he dejectedly told a friend, "There is nothing to live for now." He visited her graveside often and once said, "My heart is buried there."

Yet his grief and sorrow deepened his compassion and patience toward others, preparing him for public service. The change in him caused biographer G. Frederick Owen to remark that he now had "a sympathy, which only the unseen force of sacred sorrow can produce."

Building on his earlier candidacy, he was elected to the state House of Representatives when he was twenty-five. After

Perseverance

serving four consecutive terms in the state legislature, he made an unsuccessful bid for U.S. Congress. He was elected to the U.S. House of Representatives on his second attempt but served only one term, as he was defeated for reelection. He again faced bitter disappointment in his bid for the U.S. Senate. Although he won the popular vote, he lost the electoral vote.

During a most tumultuous time in U.S. history, he won our nation's highest office despite not appearing on the ballot in ten states. Encouraging a disheartened nation, he said, "If we have patience, if we restrain ourselves, if we allow ourselves not to run off in a passion, we still have confidence that the Almighty, the Maker of the universe, will, through the instrumentality of this great and intelligent people, bring us through this as He has other difficulties."

As the nation's conflict escalated, he fervently prayed for a speedy resolution in the Civil War. Yet he acknowledged, "If God wills that it continue...still it must be said 'the judgments of the Lord are true and righteous altogether.'

With malice toward none, with charity for all, with firmness in the right as God gives us to see the right, let us strive on to finish the work we are in."

Today, his profile remains on the U.S. penny, honoring President Abraham Lincoln's leadership and perseverance during democracy's greatest test.

Have you ever felt like giving up? Has it ever seemed that all odds were against you, that the challenges you faced were impossible? Have you ever attempted to accomplish something only to discover halfway through that the task was harder than you'd first thought – too demanding, requiring too great a sacrifice?

"Just quit," you said to yourself. But something deep within beckoned you onward. Sure, quitting seemed the easy way out, but you knew that the anguish of defeat would be greater than the struggle to finish. You wanted to give up…but you didn't!

You kept going. Through tears, through doubts, through the fog of the unknown – you determined you wouldn't give in. And surprisingly, the farther you went, the stronger you became! You stretched beyond your limitations and pursued your dream despite the odds. You held on to the purpose of your quest. And perseverance had its way, depositing deter- mination and patience into your being. You were forever changed.

Romans 5:3 reveals that "tribulation produces persever- ance; and perseverance, character; and character, hope." Wow! Could it be that the trials that come our way actually produce in us character that is pleasing to God? Perseverance produces amazing results. It was perseverance that motivated the woman with an issue of blood to "press in" and touch the hem of Jesus' garment. Perseverance is what initiated Paul and Silas's singing behind locked bars. Perseverance is what energized Noah to continue building the ark when others mocked him. And it's what propelled Esther to go before the king.

Never give up! Remember, with Christ, you can do all things! Perseverance is the rocket fuel of your heart – the fuel that launches dreams. And He's given you a ready supply.

You'll reap the rewards if you don't give up...

Courage is fear
that has said its prayers.

—DOROTHY BERNARD

Courage

Rosa Louise McCauley, born February 4, 1913, in Tuskegee, Alabama, grew up in the days of racial segregation, Jim Crow laws, and the terrorizing tactics of the Ku Klux Klan. As a child, reading Psalms 23 and 27 from the Bible encouraged her to trust in God and not to give in to fear. Prayer and Bible reading were a regular part of her childhood.

Despite the 1954 Supreme Court ruling in *Brown v. Board of Education*, which declared separate-but-equal schools unconstitutional, acts and attitudes of prejudice continued in the Deep South.

One December day in 1955, Rosa, now a married, forty-two-year-old seamstress, was riding home from work on a Montgomery bus. As usual, she'd paid her ten-cent fare at the front of the bus, gotten off the bus, then reentered through the back door. When a white man boarded the bus, the driver looked at Rosa and instructed her and other passengers to move to the rear of the bus. Rosa was already seated in the "colored" section,

Courage

but ordinances dictated that black people could not sit in the same row or across the aisle from white people.

At first, no one moved, but as the driver repeated insults and made threats, those sitting near Rosa gave in to intimidation. But Rosa quietly decided that it wasn't right for any female to be forced to give up her seat because of the color of her skin. God took away her fear, and despite imminent arrest, she remained seated, courageously refusing to relinquish her seat to the white male passenger. Even though she was aware that she might be manhandled, beaten, or lynched for her stand, Rosa trusted the Lord for strength to endure whatever she had to face.

Within five minutes, two police officers arrived and arrested Rosa. The arresting officer had no answer for Rosa's simple question: "Why do you push us around?" All he could do was reference "the law." Alone in jail, she silently prayed, unaware that her quiet defiance was setting into motion a chain of events that would forever alter racial discrimination in America. Later that evening, she was released.

Reverend Martin Luther King Jr. organized a nonviolent boycott of the city bus line the day of her trial. The standoff ended 381 days later when the U.S. Supreme Court declared Montgomery's bus segregation policy unconstitutional.

Courage

Soon after the boycott ended, Rosa rode a nonsegregated bus for the first time.

Because she had the courage to take a stand, Rosa Parks earned national recognition as the mother of the modern-day American civil-rights movement. Rosa's brave words inspire us all: "What really matters is not whether we have problems, but how we go through them. We must keep going on to make it through whatever we are facing."

When we think of courage, we all think of heroes like Superman or Zorro, whose daring feats of gallantry in the midst of danger saved the day. We also think of war heroes fighting on the front lines of battlefields.

But when God thinks of courage, He thinks of courageous women like my mom, who raised nine children. Or my friend Joanna, who stands strong in her faith while fighting a life-threatening disease. And missionaries – men and women who risk their lives in unknown lands for the cause of Christ.

And...He thinks of you. "Not me," you may say. "I'm no hero!" But think back. Remember when you were a child and stood up to the school bully because she'd talked badly about someone you loved? And just in case your courage waned, your best friend was waiting around the corner to lend you some of hers. Remember the times you said no to something you knew was wrong, even though you could have gotten away with it?

He remembers. When you took time from your busy schedule to help someone in need, when you wiped away someone's tears or made someone's day less lonely, every time you defended a friend or shone your light in someone else's darkness – on all these occasions, you've been a hero.

There's an old saying, "If you don't stand for something, you'll fall for anything." Courage lifts you up when you feel like sitting down. Courage remembers that "all things are possible with God."

Courage

In your daily battlefields, it takes courage to begin each day with a smile on your face and a song in your heart. It takes courage to share your love, your home, your creativity, and your faith.

When your cause is greater than your fear, courage prevails!

Life's bullies will always be around. But I've got great news! Your Best Friend is waiting close by just in case you need help. He's the all-powerful, super source of your courage. He's the perfect role model – the only Hero you'll ever need. His name is Jesus.

fifty-four

Take heart when you face trouble...

Joy shines in the eyes,

comes out in the speech and walk.

You cannot keep it in

for it bubbles out.

When people see the habitual

happiness in your eyes, it will make

them realize they are the

loved children of God.

—MOTHER TERESA

Write your own story of how God has filled your life with boundless hope and joy.

_____

_____

_____

_____

_____

_____

_____

_____

_____

_____

Other books that include
LeAnn Weiss's paraphrased Scriptures

Hugs for Dad
Hugs for Grandparents
Hugs for the Holidays
Hugs for the Hurting
Hugs for Mom
Hugs for Women
Hugs to Encourage and Inspire
Hugs from Heaven: Embraced by the Savior
Hugs from Heaven: On Angel Wings

Also by LeAnn Weiss

Hugs for Friends
Heartlifters™ *for Women*

fifty-eight

Sources

Over one hundred sources were used in compiling the biographical sketches in this book. The following sources were primary.

Barbara Johnson

Johnson, Barbara. *Where Does a Mother Go to Resign?* Minneapolis, Minn.: Bethany House, 1979.

———. *Splashes of Joy in the Cesspools of Life*. Dallas: Word Publishing, 1992.

Fanny Crosby

Ruffin, Bernard. *Fanny Crosby: The Hymn Writer*. Uhrichsville, Ohio: Barbour Publishing, Inc., 1995.

Woodbridge, John, ed. *Portraits of Believers from All Walks of Life*. Chicago: Moody Press, 1992.

Madeline Manning Mimms

Mimms, Madeline Manning. *The Hope of Glory*. (Her forthcoming autobiography).

Sources

Ben W. Hooper

Hooper, Ben W. *The Unwanted Boy.* Knoxville, Tenn.: The University of Tennessee Press, 1963.

Henrietta Mears

Baldwin, Ethel May, and David V. Benson. *Henrietta Mears and How She Did It.* Glendale, Calif.: Regal, 1966.

Bright, Bill. *Come Help Change the World.* San Bernardino, Calif.: Here's Life Publishers, Inc., 1985.

Roe, Earl O., ed. *Dream Big: The Henrietta Mears Story.* Ventura, Calif.: Regal, 1990.

Abraham Lincoln

Burns, Roger. *Abraham Lincoln.* New York: Chelsea House Publishers, 1986.

Owen, G. Frederick. *Abraham Lincoln: The Man and His Faith.* Wheaton, Ill.: Tyndale House Publisher, 1976.

Rosa Parks

Parks, Rosa, and Gregory J. Reed. *Quiet Strengths.* Grand Rapids, Mich.: Zondervan Publishing House, 1994.